DESIGN AND CREATE

Water Projects

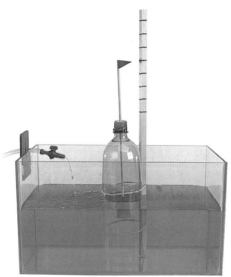

John Williams

RSVP
RAINTREE
STECK-VAUGHN
PUBLISHERS
The Steck-Vaughn Company

Austin, Texas

Published by Raintree Steck-Vaughn Publishers, an imprint of Steck-Vaughn Company

Library of Congress Cataloging-in-Publication Data
Williams, John.
Water Projects / John Williams.
    p.   cm.—(Design and create)
    Includes bibliographical references and index.
    Summary: Provides instructions for a variety of projects involving water, including a water clock, a flood alarm, and a dredger.
    ISBN 0-8172-4890-0
    1. Water—Experiments—Juvenile literature.
    [1.Water—Experiments. 2. Experiments.]
    I. Title. II. Series: Design and create.
    GB662.3.W55 1998
    532'.0078—dc21   97-20320

Printed in Italy. Bound in the United States.
1 2 3 4 5 6 7 8 9 0 02 01 00 99 98

Commissioned photography by Zul Mukhida
Cover photography by APM Studios

CONTENTS

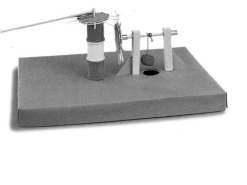

INTRODUCTION

Two-thirds of the earth's surface is covered by water. On it, ships carry cargo made in factories, dug out of the earth, or grown for food. Although people travel long distances in trains and airplanes, even today many people driving cars or trucks have to make short trips on ferryboats.

Boats and water are also used for pleasure. Visit the beach and you will see people on surfboards or water skis, in sailboats, or just swimming.

Water is very important for growing food. In some places where there is not enough rain, people have designed ingenious machines for getting water out of rivers or wells and onto the land.

Big ships carrying cargo sail all over the world. To make loading the cargo easier, it is often put into large steel boxes, called containers.

Some people live on boats, rather than on dry land. These are houseboats in Bangladesh.

For thousands of years, water has been an important source of power. Before motors were invented, water was used to drive mill wheels joined to all sorts of machines. These machines were often for grinding wheat, but there were also machines for crushing rocks and minerals. It has only been within the last 250 years that other forms of energy—such as electricity—have become available.

This book will help you design and make some of these machines and boats and learn how to use water in many helpful ways.

This water slide uses the force of running water for fun and recreation.

INFLATABLE BOAT

Some small boats are made of rubber or plastic filled with air. This makes them easy to store when they are not being used because the air can be let out and the boat can be folded up. This model is made by using a balloon and some plastic. If the balloon is hard to blow up, ask an adult to help you.

YOU WILL NEED

- Long balloon
- Plastic bubble wrap
- Plastic shipping tape
- Corrugated plastic
- Plain paper
- Felt-tip pen
- Pencil
- Scissors
- Balloon pump

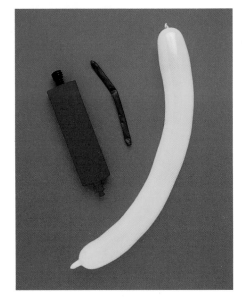

1 Ask an adult to help you to blow up the balloon, using the balloon pump. Let some air out and tie a knot at the end.

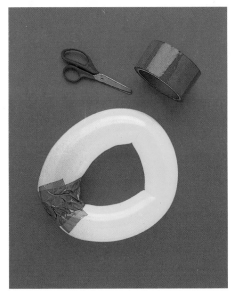

2 Bend the balloon into a circle and stick the ends together firmly with shipping tape.

Inflatable boats can be made in many different shapes. Some are used to rescue people who get into trouble at sea. Others are just for having fun, such as on vacation.

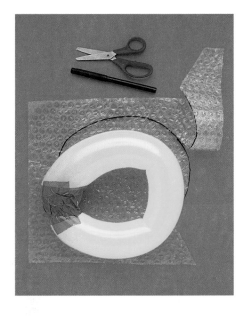

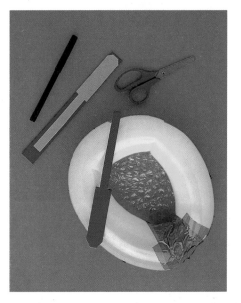

3 Put the balloon circle on the smooth side of the plastic bubble wrap. Draw around the outside with a felt-tip pen. Cut out the shape.

4 Using pieces of shipping tape, stick the base of the boat to the sides. Make sure there are no gaps, so the boat will be waterproof.

5 Design some oars to go with the boat. Draw their shape on plain paper and cut it out. Use the shape as a pattern and cut two oars from the corrugated plastic.

NOW TRY THIS

Inflatable boats are often used for life rafts if a bigger boat sinks. People in a life raft, waiting to be rescued, would need shelter from the weather. Design and make a cover to go over the boat. Make it out of something water-proof.

SHADUF

Shadufs have been used to get water out of rivers for thousands of years. Instead of lifting the water by hand, people used a shaduf— a lever plus a heavy weight—to do the work.

People made shadufs from stones and whatever else they could find around them, such as wooden logs tied together with rope. Here is a model to make that uses the same type of natural materials.

Shadufs were mostly used many years ago, before better machines were invented, but they are sometimes still seen in Middle Eastern countries such as Egypt.

YOU WILL NEED

- Forked stick, about 6 in. (15 cm) long
- Straight stick, about 10 in. (25 cm) long
- Modeling clay
- Small stones
- Netting vegetable bag
- Thin cardboard or foil
- String
- Scissors

1 Make the modeling clay into a ball. Push the forked stick into it so that it stands upright.

2 Cut a piece from the vegetable netting. Put the stones on it and tie it like a small bag.

3 Make a small bucket of cardboard or foil. Make a handle with string and tie it on.

4 Cut two pieces of string about 8 in. (20 cm) long. Take the long straight stick. Tie the bag of stones on one end and the bucket on the other.

5 Put the long stick in the fork of the other stick so that it balances. Tie it on loosely with another piece of string.

6 Try lifting some water with the bucket. When the lever is balanced, water can be lifted without much effort.

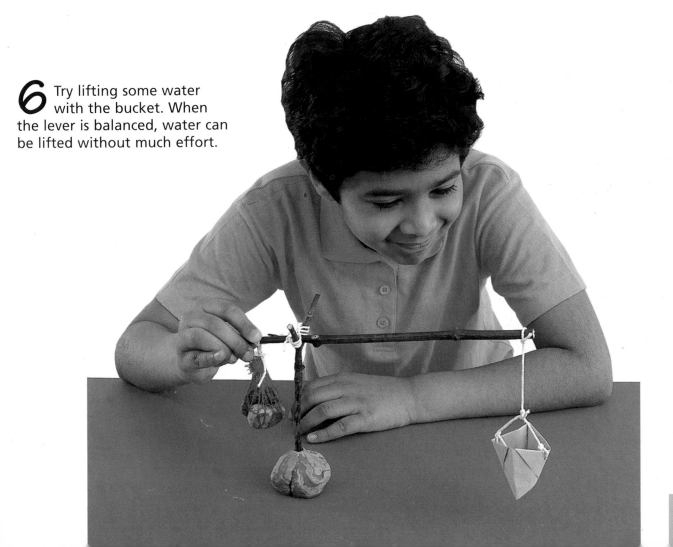

WATER CLOCK

YOU WILL NEED

- Plastic bottle
- Stiff plastic or cardboard
- Wooden dowel, about .25 in. (5 mm) diameter, a little longer than bottle
- Thread spool
- .25 x .25 in. (5 x 5 mm) strip wood, about twice the length of bottle
- Rubber bands
- Masking tape
- Glue
- Pen or pencil
- Scissors
- Ruler
- Hole punch
- Small hacksaw
- Waterproof container
- Plastic tube and tap (optional)

People first found a way of measuring time about 1500 B.C. They made sundials, which used shadows made by the sun. However, sundials could not work at night or on cloudy days, so another way of telling the time was needed. Water clocks were used until clocks with pendulums were invented, in the 1600s.

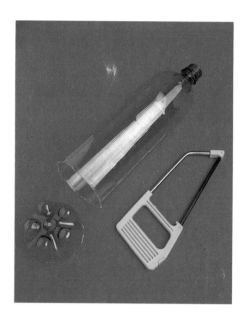

1 Ask an adult to help you cut off the bottom of the bottle, using the hacksaw.

2 Stand the bottle on the cardboard or plastic and draw around it. Draw a slightly smaller circle inside this and cut it out. Make a small hole in the center.

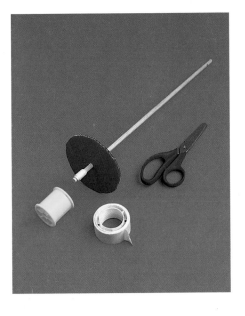

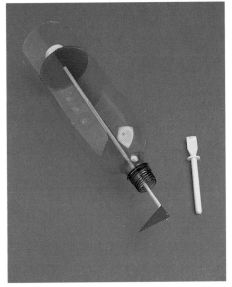

3 Push the circle onto the dowel. It should fit tightly. Wind some masking tape around the end of the dowel. Push the spool over the masking tape and make sure it fits tightly.

4 Push the other end of the dowel through the top of the bottle. Make a small pointer out of cardboard and glue it on the top. Let the glue dry.

5 Join the piece of strip wood to the bottle with two or three rubber bands. Stand the water clock in a waterproof container.

6 Let water run or drip down and watch the pointer rise up. Measure how fast it moves against a clock, and mark intervals on the length of wood.

NOW TRY THIS

Make another type of water clock that is like an alarm clock. It uses a balloon and a pin. Put the blown-up balloon at the top of the length of strip wood. Put the pin pointing upward on the dowel. When the dowel gets to the top, the pin bursts the balloon.

WATERWHEEL

YOU WILL NEED

- Two thick cardboard circles, about 2.5 in. (6 cm) diameter, with small center holes

- Eight pieces wooden dowel, about .25 in. (6 mm) diameter and 2 in. (5 cm) long

- Four pieces corrugated plastic, each 2 x 2 in. (5 x 5 cm)

- Waxed drink carton

- One piece wooden dowel, .25 in. (6 mm) diameter and 3 in. (7.5cm) longer than width of carton

- Two pieces plastic tubing, .25 in. (6 mm) diameter and .5 in. (1 cm) long, slit down the side

- Thread

- Modeling clay

- Glue

- Hole punch

- Pencil & pencil sharpener

- Ruler

- Scissors

Falling water has energy that can make objects move. Before electricity was discovered, water was used to drive machines. Today, we use the power of water to drive generators and make electricity.

The Laxey Wheel was built in 1854 on the Isle of Man, part of Great Britain. It was designed to pump water out of nearby mines. It has a diameter of 72 ft. (22 m), and is the biggest waterwheel in the world.

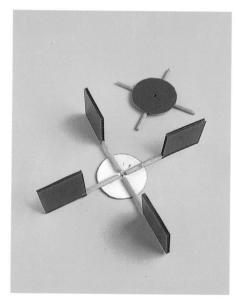

1 Divide the cardboard circles into four equal parts, drawing lines with a pencil and ruler. Glue a piece of dowel along each line, so they stick out the same distance at each end. Let the glue dry.

2 Take one of the cardboard and dowel circles. Push a piece of plastic onto the end of each dowel. It may help to sharpen the dowels a little first with a pencil sharpener.

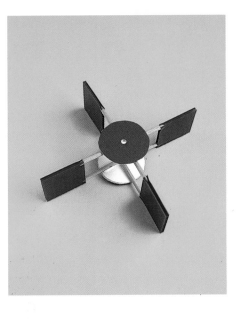

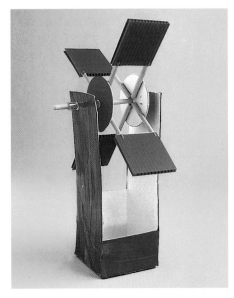

3 Take the other circle and do the same, so the the two circles are joined.

4 Cut off the top and two opposite sides of the carton. Make two holes in the other sides, opposite each other. They must be big enough so the dowel can turn freely.

5 Push the long dowel through a hole in the carton, then through the waterwheel, and out the other side. Make it longer on one side than the other. Hold it in place with the pieces of plastic tubing.

6 Tie a piece of thread to the long end of the dowel axle and fix a weight (such as a lump of modeling clay) to the other end of the thread. Put the waterwheel under a stream of water.

NOW TRY THIS

Attach a spool on the long end of the waterwheel axle. Make sure it fits tightly. Stick the end of the thread to the spool. See if the weight moves faster or slower.

13

FLAT-BOTTOM FERRY

YOU WILL NEED

- Waxed drink carton
- Stiff cardboard
- Four paper clips
- Two metal paper fasteners
- 3-in. (8-cm) wooden dowel, about .25 in. (6 mm) diameter
- Thread spool
- Two small pieces plastic tubing, about .25 in. (6 mm) diameter, slit down the side
- Shipping tape
- Thick thread
- Scissors and ruler
- Hole punch

People often need to cross rivers, but rivers do not always have bridges over them. Ferries with flat bottoms can cross rivers carrying cars, animals, and people. This sort of ferry is usually joined to a metal cable. An engine on the ferry winds the cable around a pulley that pulls the ferry across the river.

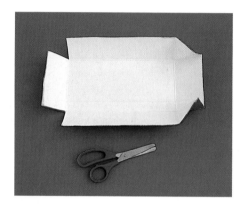

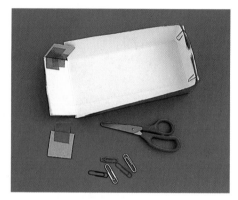

1 Cut the carton in half lengthwise. One end should open out and fold up neatly. Make a cut down the other two corners and fold the end out flat.

2 Cut two squares of cardboard to fit the carton sides (see picture). Stick them to the flat ends with shipping tape and fold them on the join. Fold both ends up again and hold them in place with paper clips.

Flat ferries have a ramp at each end so that people can get on at one side of the river and walk or drive off at the other. This ferry is in China.

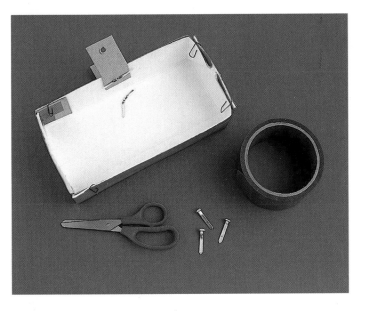

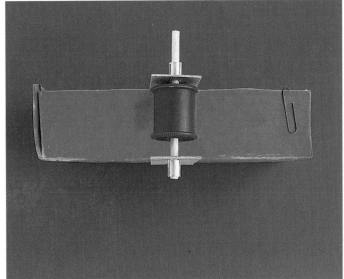

3 Cut two rectangles of stiff cardboard, about 1 x 2 in. (3 x 6 cm). Make a .25-in. (5-mm) hole in each one, about .5 in. (1.5 cm) from the end. Fold one piece in half. Join the folded one to the side and the straight one to the bottom, using paper fasteners.

4 Wind some masking tape around the middle of the dowel. Push a spool over the masking tape, so it fits tightly. Push the ends of the dowel through the two holes in the cardboard. Put a piece of tubing on each end to hold the dowel in place.

5 Join the thread to the edge of a water container, wind it around the spool once and join it to the opposite side. It should not be too tight. Turn the dowel with your fingers and the ferry will go across the water. Either end of the ferry can go down to let cars on and off.

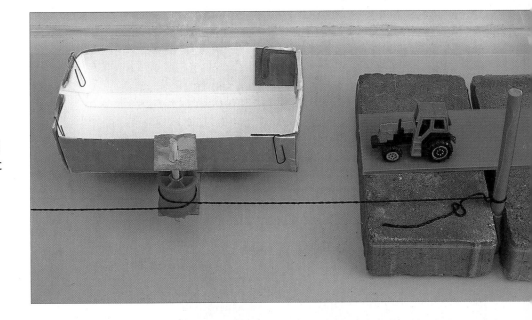

NOW TRY THIS

Make a handle for the winch that winds the cable around the pulley. Cut a circle of cardboard about 2 in. (5 cm) diameter. Punch a small hole in the center, and another hole near the edge. Glue a small piece of dowel in the hole near the edge. Glue the center hole on the top of the dowel that goes through the spool.

TORPEDO FISH

YOU WILL NEED

- Small plastic drink bottle with screw-on lid about 9 in. (23 cm) high
- Plastic propeller, about 6 in. (15 cm) long
- Piece of corrugated plastic, about 4 x 12 in. (10 x 30 cm).
- Several thick rubber bands
- Medium paper clip
- Small plastic bead
- Small piece of dowel
- Bradawl

Be careful when using a bradawl to make holes.

- **Hold the object in a vise if possible.**
- **Ask an adult to show you what to do.**

This project works a little like a torpedo and also like a fish. The energy stored in a wound-up rubber band drives the fish along, and the fin keeps the body even in the water.

1 Use the bradawl to make a hole in the middle of the bottom of the plastic bottle. Also make a hole in the bottle top.

2 Unbend the paper clip, leaving a hook in one end. Push the other end through the bottle top, bead, and propeller. Bend the end of the paper clip tightly over the center of the propeller.

Fish have fins on their bodies—at the top and bottom, on the sides, and on their tails. They use their fins to move themselves along and to steer.

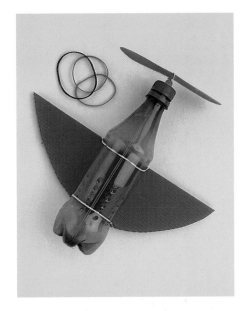

3 Tie a piece of string to a rubber band. Push the string through the hole in the bottom of the bottle. Put the dowel through the rubber band and pull the rest of the band through the bottle.

4 Hook the rubber band onto the paper clip in the bottle top. Cut the string off and screw the top back on the bottle.

5 Cut a fin from a piece of balsa wood or corrugated plastic. It should have one curved side, about 4 in. (10 cm) at its widest point. Join it to the bottle with rubber bands.

6 Undo the top a little and let the bottle half fill with water. Tighten the top again. Wind up the propeller as far as possible, and let it go in the water.

CATAMARAN

YOU WILL NEED

- Small plastic drink bottle about 9 in. (23 cm) high

- Piece of balsa wood, .25 in. (6 mm) thick and 2 x 11 in. (5 x 28 cm)

- Three pieces of dowel, about .25 in. (6 mm) diameter and same length as plastic bottle

- Piece of dowel, about .25 in. (6 mm) diameter and 14 in. (35 cm) long

- Thread spool

- 12 rubber bands

- Thread

- Tissue paper, fabric, or plastic (for sail)

- Masking tape and glue

- Small hacksaw

- Drill with .25 in. (6 mm) drill bit

Most boats have one hull that floats on the water. A catamaran has two hulls that make it wider and harder to tip over when it is sailing.

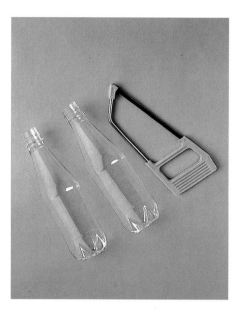

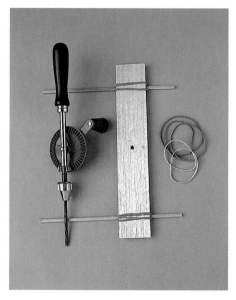

1 Ask an adult to help you cut the plastic bottle in half lengthwise, using the hacksaw. Hold the bottle in a vise if possible.

2 Drill a hole in the center of the balsa wood. Using rubber bands, join two pieces of dowel to the balsa wood, on either side of the hole.

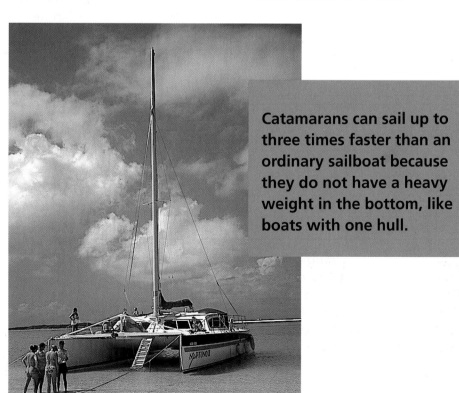

Catamarans can sail up to three times faster than an ordinary sailboat because they do not have a heavy weight in the bottom, like boats with one hull.

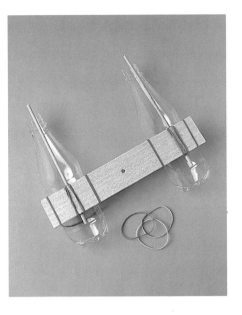

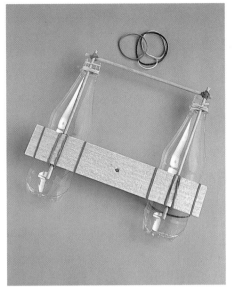

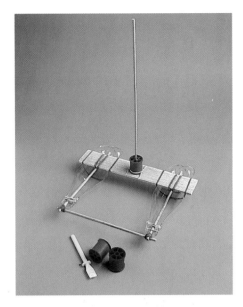

3 Put the balsa wood and dowels over the plastic bottle halves. Join the balsa to the bottles with more rubber bands. Make sure the bottles are the same distance from each end of the balsa wood.

4 Wind rubber bands around the neck ends of the bottles. Join the third piece of dowel to the others, at right angles. Use more rubber bands to hold them together.

5 Put the spool over the hole in the balsa wood. Hold it in place with another rubber band. Put some glue on the end of the mast and push it down into the hole in the wood. Let the glue dry.

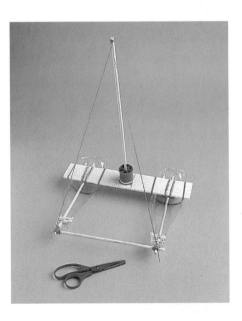

7 Make a sail out of paper, plastic, or fabric. It should be in the shape of a triangle. Stick the top of the sail to the mast with a little glue, and the bottom corners to the rigging with masking tape.

6 Add some rigging to make the mast stronger. Tie a thread to one side of the front of the boat, then the top of the mast and down to the other side. Make sure it is tight.

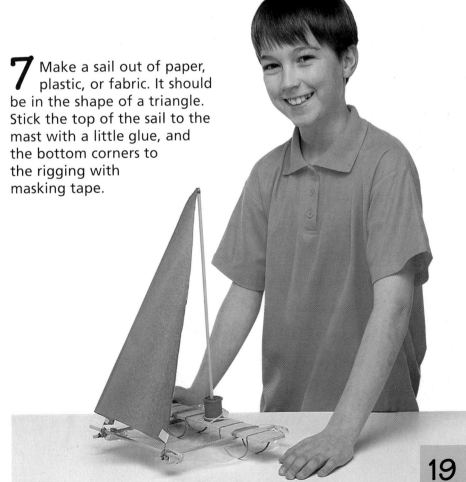

PADDLEBOAT

Be careful when using a bradawl to make holes. See page 16.

Paddleboats were first built about 200 years ago. Sometimes they had a paddle wheel on either side, and others used one paddle at the back, like this model.

YOU WILL NEED

- Square-shaped plastic bottle, about 10 in. (25 cm) high
- Two pieces .25 x .25 in. (6 x 6 mm) strip wood, about 1.5 times length of bottle
- Small piece of dowel, about 1 in. (2.5 cm) longer than width of bottle
- Thread spool
- Recycled plastic food container lids
- Eight thin rubber bands
- One long thick rubber band
- Masking tape
- Scissors and ruler
- Plain paper
- Marker pen that will draw on plastic
- Stapler
- Bradawl

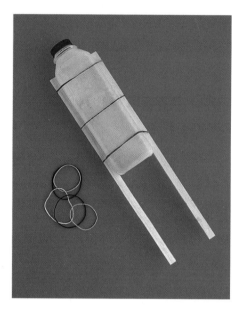

1 Put the pieces of strip wood on either side of the plastic bottle. Hold them together with several rubber bands.

2 Draw the paddle shape on paper to make a pattern. It should look like a fat T shape. Make the top of the T the same width as the spool. Use the paper pattern to mark out four shapes on the plastic lids. Cut the paddles out.

3 Stick the plastic paddles onto the spool with masking tape. Make sure there is the same space between each one. Wind a rubber band around each side to hold them in place.

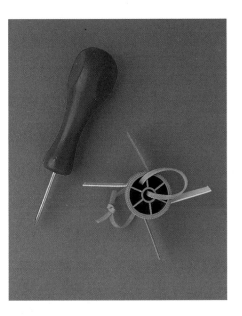

4 Ask an adult to help you use the bradawl to make a hole down one side of the spool. Cut the thick rubber band and thread it through both holes. Tie it together again.

Paddleboats were mostly used on lakes and rivers in the 1800s. They did not work well on rough water, such as the sea.

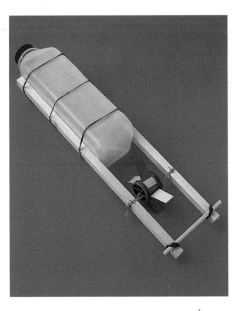

5 Put the rubber band over the ends of the wood and slide it up toward the bottle. Staple the rubber band to the wood at the sides. Put the dowel across the ends of the wood. Join them together tightly with rubber bands.

6 Wind the spool, many times, toward the back of the boat. Put the boat in the water and let go.

NOW TRY THIS

Make a motor-driven paddleboat. Fix the spool on a dowel axle. Mount a small electric motor (1.5V–4.5V) and 4.5V battery on top of the bottle. Join the spindle of the motor to the spool with a rubber band.

SAKIA

YOU WILL NEED

- Top of a shoe box

- Two pieces of .25 x .25 in. (6 x 6 mm) strip wood, about 3 in. (8 cm) long

- Two or three spools

- Three wooden dowels, .25 in. (6 mm) diameter: one 4 in. (10 cm), one 4.75 in. (12 cm), one 7 in. (18 cm) long

- Four cardboard circles 1.5 in. (4 cm) diameter with small center holes

- Toothpicks or matchsticks

- Small pieces of plastic tubing, about .25 in. (6 mm) diameter, slit down the side

- Thread

- Glue and scissors

- Pencil and ruler

- Drill with .25 in. (6 mm) drill bit

This sakia in Egypt is being turned by a cow, which walks around and around in a circle all day. The sakia turns the wheel with the pots on it. The pots scoop the water and pour it into a stream that runs onto the fields.

This is a simple machine that uses two special wheels called cogs to get water out of a deep well. The cogs are made of cardboard circles and toothpicks. They must be put on very carefully so that the distance between each stick is exactly the same.

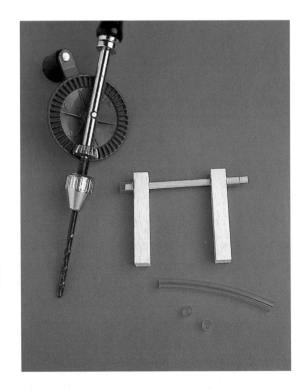

1 Ask an adult to help you drill a hole through each piece of strip wood, about .5 in. (1.25 cm) from one end. Push the 4-in. (10-cm) piece of dowel through and make sure it can turn freely. Put a piece of tubing on each end.

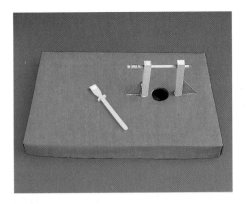

2 Cut a hole about 1 in. (3 cm) diameter in the box top. Glue the wood to either side of the hole. Glue small cardboard triangles at the bottom to hold the wood more firmly. Let the glue dry.

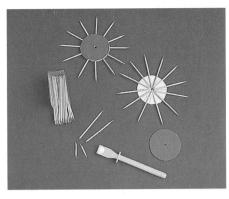

3 Divide each cardboard circle into four, and then into twelve. Glue a stick on each line. When the glue is dry, glue a second cardboard circle on top.

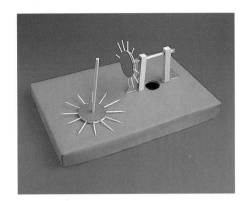

4 Put a cog on the end of the axle over the hole. You may have to break off the ends of the sticks so that the cog will fit. Put the other cog on the end of the 4.75-in. (12-cm) dowel. Put some glue on the holes to stick the cogs on the dowels.

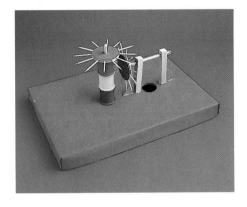

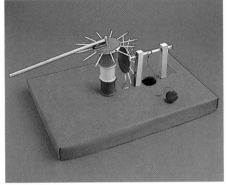

7 When all the glue has dried, turn the long dowel. The axle over the hole will turn and bring up the "bucket" out of the well.

5 Glue three spools together. Put them on the box, and put the dowel and cog down the center hole. Figure out where to put the spools so that the cogs just meet. Then glue the bottom spool to the box.

6 Glue the last piece of dowel to the top of the cog in the spools. You may have to add some small pieces of cardboard to make it high enough. Tie some thread to the axle over the hole. Put a weight, such as modeling clay, on the end of the thread.

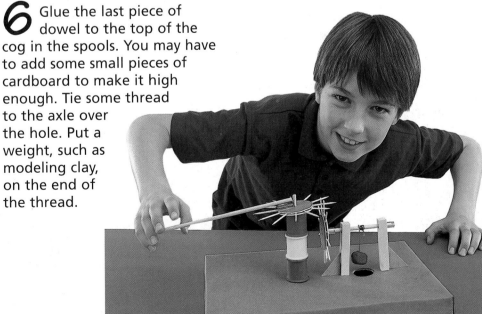

DREDGER

YOU WILL NEED

- Two 12-in. (30-cm) and six 2.5-in. (6-cm) pieces of .25 x .25 in. (6 x 6 mm) strip wood
- Four small cardboard triangles
- Four pieces wooden dowel, .25 in. (6 mm) diameter: two 6 in. (15 cm), one 7 in. (18 cm), one 1 in. (3 cm) long
- Thread spool
- Rubber bands
- Piece of plastic bottle
- Two plastic bottles
- Thick thread
- Small pieces of plastic tubing about .25 in. (6 mm) diameter, slit down side
- Glue
- Ruler and pencil
- Drill with .25 in. (6 mm) drill bit

Sometimes rivers and harbors get clogged with mud or sand. This keeps boats from going along because the water is not deep enough. To make the water deep again, a machine called a dredger is used to scoop out the soil or sand and put it somewhere else.

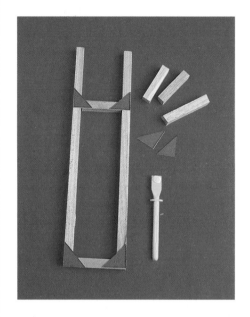

1 Take the two 12-in. (30-cm) pieces of strip wood and two 2.5-in. (6-cm) pieces and make the frame as shown in the photograph. Glue it together. Glue the cardboard triangles over the joins to make them stronger.

2 Take the other four pieces of strip wood. In each piece drill a hole about .5 in. (1 cm) from one end. (Ask an adult to help you with the drill.) Glue two pieces at each end of the long frame. The pieces should be about 2 in. (5 cm) from the end.

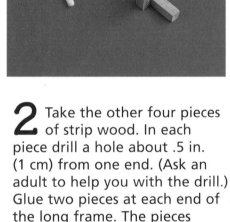

There are many different types of dredgers. Some grab the mud, like the one in this photo. Some use many buckets joined to a chain made into a circle, and others suck up the mud through a big tube.

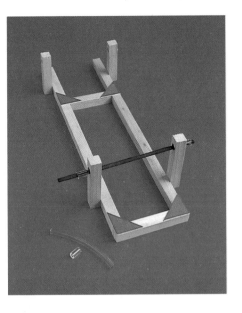

3 At the closed end of the frame, push a 6-in. (15-cm) piece of dowel through the holes in the two uprights. Put pieces of tubing on each end to hold it in place.

4 Take the other 6-in. (15-cm) dowel. Push it through a hole in the strip wood, the spool, and the other piece of wood. Put some glue on the holes in the wood. Add pieces of tubing on either side of the spool to keep it in the center.

5 Make the scoop. Take the 7-in. (18-cm) piece of dowel. Cut a T-shaped piece of plastic. Fold up two sides of the plastic and join them to the dowel with rubber bands.

6 Join the scoop to the spool with a rubber band so that it faces outward. Cut a piece of thread about 12 in. (30 cm) long. Tie one end to the scoop shaft and the other end to the dowel.

7 Join the dredger to the two plastic bottles with rubber bands. Float the dredger in some water. Tie it to the sides to keep it from moving when it is being used. Wind the handle and the scoop will lift.

FLOOD ALARM

During heavy rain, rivers and even dams may burst their banks, and many houses and farms are flooded. People need a warning if this is going to happen so that they can move to higher ground. This project shows how to make an electric alarm that tells you when the water level is getting high.

YOU WILL NEED

- Plastic tube approx 1.5 in. (4 cm) diameter
- Cork with diameter a little smaller than tube
- 3 ft. (1 m) single-core electrical wire
- Buzzer (or light bulb and bulb holder)
- Battery (4.5V minimum)
- Aluminum kitchen foil
- Tape
- Plastic shipping tape
- Scissors
- Wire stripper and cutter
- Small hacksaw
- Sink or tank same depth as or deeper than the length of the tube

Because a big dam holds so much water, it could be very dangerous if it overflowed. An alarm would tell people when the water was getting near the top of the wall.

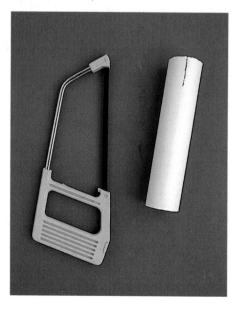

1 Ask an adult to help you use the hacksaw to cut a slit, about 1 in. (3 cm) deep, at the top of the plastic tube. Use a vise to hold the tube while you are cutting it.

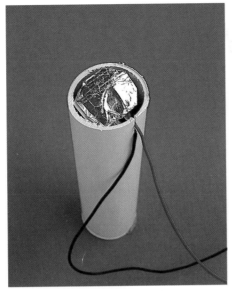

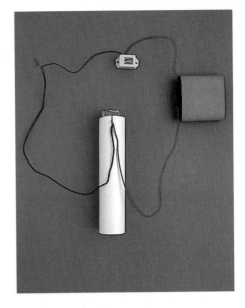

2 Cut two pieces of wire. Strip about 1 in. (2 cm) of plastic from each end. Cut two pieces of foil, small enough to fit in the tube, and attach them with tape to one end of the pieces of wire.

3 Slide the wires into the slit so that the two pieces of foil are at the top of the tube, one over the other. They should be close, but not touching.

4 Put the ends of the buzzer wires on the battery terminals to find out which way it works. Join one buzzer wire to the battery, and the other to one of the loose wires. Join the other loose wire to the other battery terminal.

6 Slowly fill the sink or tank. As the water rises, the cork will float up the tube. When it reaches the top it will push the two pieces of foil together. When they touch, the buzzer will sound.

5 Tape the tube to the side of a sink or tank with plastic tape. Fill the tank so that the water comes just to the bottom of the tube. Put the cork in the bottom of the tube.

27

DRINK MACHINE

YOU WILL NEED

- Strong cardboard box, such as a shoe box, about 5 x 10 x 12 in. (12 x 25 x 30 cm)
- Stiff cardboard
- 6 in. (15 cm) of .25 x .25 in. (6 x 6 mm) strip wood
- Wooden dowel, about .25 in. (6 mm) diameter and 2 in. (5 cm) longer than depth of box
- Two plastic cups, cut down to half their size
- Funnel (or cut-off end of plastic squeeze bottle)
- 6 in. (15 cm) of plastic tubing to fit end of funnel/bottle
- Narrow cardboard tube
- Pushpins and Thread
- Marbles
- Modeling clay
- Metal paper fasteners
- Glue and tape
- Scissors and ruler
- Drill with .25 in. (6 mm) drill bit

Here is an interesting machine that provides a drink when you drop a weight in the top of the box. A machine like this was first figured out by a famous Greek inventor named Hero, who lived more than 2,000 years ago.

Machines are used to sell many different things, from candy and drinks to train tickets and maps. These machines are outside a store in Japan.

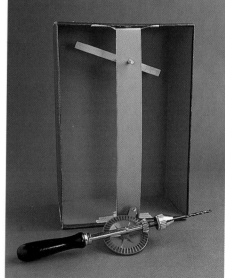

1 Cut a piece of stiff cardboard about 2 in. (5 cm) longer than the box and about 1 in. (2.5 cm) wide. Fold over 1 in. (2.5 cm) at either end. Glue it at either end so it runs down the center of the box on the open side.

2 Ask an adult to help you drill a hole through the middle of the strip wood. Make .25-in. (6-mm) holes in the box and the cardboard strip. They should be about 2 in. (5 cm) from the top of the box and opposite each other. Push the dowel through a hole, the strip wood, and out the other hole.

3 Pin a cup to one end of the wood. Cut a thread about 3 in. (7.5 cm) long. Join a small piece of modeling clay to one end of it. Pin the top of the thread to the other end of the wood.

4 Make a small hole in the bottom of the other cup. Join it to the side of the box with a paper fastener. Put a piece of tubing on the bottom of the funnel. Fix the funnel under the cup. Make a hole in the side of the box for the tube.

5 Make a hole in the top of the box for the cardboard tube. It should be over the left-hand cup.

NOW TRY THIS

● **Think of a way to refill the cup.**

● **Design a cistern or water supply to keep refilling the cup.**

6 Make sure the plasticine weight is firmly covering the hole in the bottom of the cup. Fill it about half full of water. Put another cup under the end of the tube. Drop a marble or two down the cardboard tube at the top, and your drink will come out at the bottom.

GLOSSARY

alarm   Something that makes a sound at a set time or when danger is near.

axle   A wood or metal rod on which a wheel turns.

balanced   Keeping a steady position, without falling over.

cable   A strong metal wire, used for electricity or to pull heavy loads.

cargo   Goods, not people, carried by ships, trains, aircraft, or land transport.

cog   A wheel that has teeth sticking out from it, to turn another wheel.

diameter   The distance across the center of a circle, from one side to the other.

dredging   Digging out mud or sand from underwater.

energy   Usable power that enables things, such as machines or animals, to do work.

fin   The parts of a fish that stick out from the main body. Machines can also have fins.

flood   Overflowing of water over land that is normally dry.

inflatable   Able to be pumped up with air; a tire is inflatable.

hull   The part of a boat or ship that floats in the water.

lever   A bar that can be used to move something by pushing or pulling.

load   A weight that something, such as a person, a truck, or a ship has to carry.

mast   A long pole on a boat or ship that holds up the sails.

paddle   An oar or paddle that moves or is moved by water.

pulley   A special wheel around which a rope is pulled to raise a weight or move an object.

ramp   A straight slope that joins two different heights.

template   A shape used to mark and cut out a number of the same shapes.

terminal   The part of a battery where other things—such as wires—can be joined to it.

torpedo   An object, shaped like a bottle, or like the weapon fired from a submarine toward a ship.

triangle   A shape with three sides.

tube   A long hollow round shape, usually open at both ends.

volt (V)   A measurement of the "push" or force of electricity.

waterproof   Treated so that water will not pass through it.

BOOKS TO READ

Armbruster, Ann. *Floods* (First Books–Science.) Danbury, CT: Franklin Watts, 1996.

Cossi, Olga. *Water Wars: The Fight to Control and Conserve Nature's Most Precious Resource.* Parsippany, NJ: Silver Burdett Press, 1993.

Crosher, Judith. *Technology in the Time of Ancient Egypt.* Austin, TX: Raintree Steck-Vaughn, 1997.

Fiarotta, Noel & Phyllis Fiarotta. *Water Science, Water Fun: Great Things to Do With H$_2$O.* New York: Sterling, 1996.

Kentley, Eric. *Boat* (Eyewitness Guides.) New York: Knopf Books for Young Readers, 1992.

Lauber, Patricia. *Flood: Wrestling with the Mississippi.* Washington, DC: National Geographic Children's Press, 1996.

ADDITIONAL NOTES

Inflatable Boat With a little help, this simple boat is well within the capability of even the youngest children, although children under eight should be supervised while inflating the balloons. Such boats are used as life rafts in airplanes and ships, and children can be asked to invent special menus for survivors.

Shaduf This simple device is based on the principle of the lever, which has the load at one end, effort exerted at the other, and the fulcrum somewhere in between.

Water Clock The ancient Egyptians were known to have used very accurate shadow clocks from about 1450 B.C., but it was much later that the Egyptian inventor Ctesibius built a workable water clock or clepsydra, on which this model is based.

Waterwheel Until the advent of steam, the waterwheel provided the main source of power for any kind of small industry. This is one of many designs that children can make.

Flat-Bottom Ferry The design of the hull for this boat allows for the drive-on, drive-off loading that most ferries use. This kind of chain-link ferry has no direct motive power of its own, and is therefore used only for short distances.

Torpedo Fish Most ships are driven through the water by a propeller, and the more of it that is underwater the better. Children can experiment to see how deep they can make the fish lie in the water.

Catamaran This model can be developed further by the addition of a rudder or by a change of sail rig. Most yachts use a fore-and-aft rig, and this can be made using a small length of dowel for the boom.

Paddleboat This basic design works well over short distances. Children should be encouraged to find ways to increase the power of the paddle to give the boat a greater range or to carry a heavier load.

Sakia Unlike the shaduf, which is used for lifting water over a short distance, the sakia is a mechanism for use with a deep well. Care needs to be taken when making the cogs. The spokes must be evenly spaced and it helps if they are of equal length.

Dredger This model is based on a design widely used in seventeenth-century Europe. The power was provided by one man, often working a treadmill. The dredger was floated on a pontoon made of two barges; for this model two plastic bottles have been used.

Flood Alarm Although this model suggests a way to avoid a possible catastrophe, it could just as easily be used to keep a sink from overflowing.

Drink Machine This machine also includes a lever. The weight is the plug in the water cup, and the effort is provided by the falling weight. The challenge in developing this machine is to design a method to refill the cup. The weight of water could be used to replug the cup, or perhaps a kind of cistern could be designed similar to that used in Hero's original machine.

INDEX

© Copyright 1997 Wayland (Publishers) Ltd.

Acknowledgments

The author and publishers wish to thank the following for their kind assistance with this book:
models Suhyun Haw, Yasmin Mukhida, Toby Roycroft, and Ranga Silva. Also Gabriella Casemore,
Zul Mukhida, Ruth Raudsepp, Philippa Smith, and Gus Ferguson.

For the use of their library photographs, grateful thanks are due to Chapel Studios p21 (John Heinrich),
p28 (Tim Garrod); Eye Ubiquitous p4 (D Cumming), p14 (J Waterlow), p18 (P Seheult), p22, p26
(L Fordyce); James Davis Travel Photography, p16; Topham Picturepoint p12, p24 (JT).
All other photographs belong to the Wayland Picture Library: p5 (top and bottom), p6; artwork on p8.